Contents

Cause and Effect

'Cause and effect' is a way of describing how one event leads to another. Often, the second event leads to a third and so on, creating a whole string of events.

You will be able to think of examples from your own life ...

Cause:
You stay round your friend's house for one extra game of 'Just Dance'.

Effect 1:
Because you are a bit late leaving, you get caught in a rain shower.

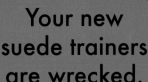

Your new suede trainers are wrecked.

Of course, the chain of cause and effect may not end there:

Effect 2:
The extra dance practice pays off when you score a big role in your school's next show.

Cause, Effect and Chaos!

In the Animal Kingdom

Author Paul Mason
with artwork by Mark Ruffle

Published in paperback in Great Britain in 2020 by Wayland
Copyright © Hodder and Stoughton, 2018

Series editor: Paul Rockett
Series design and illustration: Mark Ruffle
www.rufflebrothers.com

ISBN 978 1 5263 0579 4

Printed in China

Wayland, an imprint of
Hachette Children's Group
Part of Hodder and Stoughton
Carmelite House
50 Victoria Embankment
London EC4Y 0DZ

An Hachette UK Company
www.hachette.co.uk

In the animal kingdom, cause and effect is sometimes a matter of life and death.

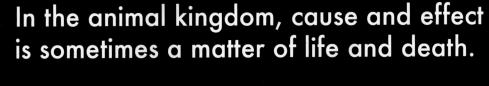

October 10

April 10

Brown snowshoe hares start growing a new coat around 10 October. The coat is white: camouflage for the snowy winter.

When the snow begins to melt on about 10 April, the hares start to grow a brown coat again. It is their summer camouflage.

Unfortunately, though, the hares' timing is not always perfect.

Lynx

Some years, the snow comes late or spring comes early.
The hares change colour out of time with their surroundings.

This can cause **chaos** and put the hares' lives in danger.

They stand out against the wrong-coloured background for every predator to see.

The Crazy-ant Menace!

Every year at the same time on Christmas Island in the Indian Ocean, the ground is carpeted in red crabs.

Millions of Christmas Island red crabs leave their burrows in the forest floor. They are heading for the sea to breed. Their journey is a perilous one.

The wet season signals the crabs to emerge from their underground homes.

The first danger they face is sunshine.

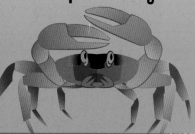

Crabs must stay moist to survive: if the sun appears, they dry out.

Some crabs hide from the sun under rocks or plants.

As the red crabs head for the sea, giant robber crabs pounce and eat some.

Millions escape – but they are not safe yet ...

Around a hundred years ago, yellow crazy ants were introduced onto Christmas Island. The population of crazy ants has grown to billions!

The yellow crazy ants spray acid into the crabs' eyes and joints. The crabs become immobile ant food.

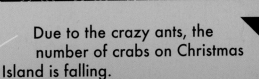

Due to the crazy ants, the number of crabs on Christmas Island is falling.

This is causing **chaos** for the island. Without crab burrows, the soil changes. Different plants start to grow, affecting the other animals that live there.

To combat the ant menace, tiny wasps have been introduced. Scientists think the wasps will quickly control ant numbers.

Salmon Spawners

Every summer, millions of salmon leave the sea and head upriver. They are going back to where they spawned, to reproduce before they die.

On Kodiak Island in Alaska, hungry bears lie in wait – or at least, they should do.

The salmon enter the river and begin to swim upstream.

Bears gather at the best fishing places.

The biggest bears
get the best fishing spots.

The bears eat as much salmon as possible, ready for winter hibernation, when they will live off their body's store of energy.

Uneaten bits of salmon are left in the nearby forests. They rot and add nutrients to the soil.

Summers on Kodiak Island have been getting warmer. This is causing chaos!

Bears love elderberries.
They have been eating those instead of salmon.

Red elderberries
now ripen earlier, at the same time as the salmon arrive.

Most salmon die after spawning. Instead of being eaten by bears, their bodies just float off downstream.

The soil no longer gets nutrients from salmon carcasses.
It becomes harder for plants to grow – including the elderberries the bears love so much. The forest animals end up with less to eat.

The Quiet Killer

Barn owls hunt mostly in the dark. They are deadly hunters and catch their prey about 75 per cent of the time.

Compare this with, for example, lions (where the success rate is 30 per cent) or peregrine falcons (47 per cent). What is it that makes barn owls such good hunters?

The hunt begins with the owl flying quietly along, listening for prey.

The owl's disc-like face funnels sound to the owl's ear, so it hears if the prey moves. It drops down head first. Even now, the owl's victim may not hear it coming.

Ear

When it hears a vole, mouse or rat, the owl hovers above until it is sure where the prey is.

At the last minute, the owl swings its talons through to grab its victim.

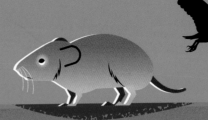

Barn owls do sometimes miss
– and they have other problems too, because modern farms are changing.

Farms have fewer old, wooden buildings for owls to roost in.

Poisons that are used to kill rats and other rodents remain in their bodies and can poison owls that eat them.

Today, the number of barn owls has fallen. Some experts think there are less than half as many as a hundred years ago.

11

Tigers that Come for Dinner

In the forests of South Asia, the Bengal tiger is an apex predator. It hunts whatever meat it can kill, but nothing – except humans – hunts tigers.

Tigers hunt mostly deer and wild cattle, but they also kill wild boar, monkeys and other animals.

The tiger sees or smells prey nearby. It makes sure it is downwind, so the victim will not smell it coming.

The tiger creeps closer.

Its specially flexible shoulders allow it to walk with its belly almost on the ground.

When the tiger is close enough, it races forwards.
Tigers can sprint 50 kph over short distances.

The tiger aims
to bite its prey
on the neck,
crushing its
windpipe.
The prey
suffocates.

Elderly or sick tigers are too slow to catch normal
prey such as deer.

They have to find something slower for their
dinner – such as *local villagers!*

In South Asia, about a hundred people a
year are attacked and killed by tigers.

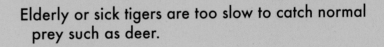

The Dragon's Bite

There are no actual fire-breathing dragons in the world. The closest thing we have is a giant* lizard known as a Komodo dragon, from Indonesia.

The Komodo's breath may not be fiery, but it is foul. And this dragon is dangerous – to large animals, and to humans.

The Komodo dragon lies in wait for its victims. Its brown skin is good camouflage among the plants and rocks.

The dragon flicks out its tongue to sense approaching victims – including people.

Komodos have poor hearing and vision, but a good sense of smell. They use their forked tongue to 'taste' the air and find out who's around.

*Komodo dragons can reach 3 m long and weigh 70 kg.

When the prey is close enough, the dragon lunges forwards and seizes it in its jaws.

Komodo dragons can run at up to 20 kph.

which can smell blood and rotting flesh from 8 km away.

The smell of blood attracts other dragons …

If the prey pulls free and escapes, the bite keeps bleeding. It contains **anticoagulants,** and may be poisonous.

Eventually, the poison takes effect and the bitten prey becomes weak and collapses.

When this happens … the Komodo dragons are waiting.

Polar Peril!

Each spring in the Arctic, polar bears leave their winter hibernation. They head for the sea ice to hunt seals.

The bears need to eat plenty over the coming months, to build up energy reserves for their next hibernation.

Bears sniff out food.

The bear heads for the hole, then waits patiently for the seal to come up for a breath.

A bear can smell a seal at a breathing hole a kilometre away.

As the seal surfaces, the bear pounces.

More often than not, the seal escapes.

Some bears come looking for food on land. Their white coats are not camouflaged, so hunting is tricky.

There is food around human settlements, but bear-human contact is dangerous for both sides. Many bears have been shot, and a few people have been **killed by bears.**

Bears need to make lots of attacks and hunt over a large area. But our planet is getting warmer. **There is less ice in the Arctic,** so the polar bears' hunting ground is shrinking.

The ice melts sooner and forms later each year.

The bears find it harder to store up fat reserves for winter.

The Snake that Stuffs Itself

When baby boa constrictors are born, they are about 40 cm long. They hunt small creatures such as mice. But boa constrictors never stop growing ...

By 25 years old, some boa constrictors are nearly 4 m long! A snake that big can hunt almost anything.

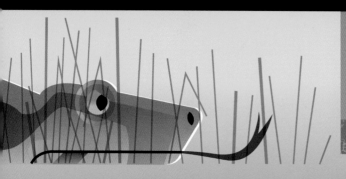

The snake hides, flicking out its tongue to taste the air for prey.

As the prey gets closer it causes vibrations in the ground and air, which the snake feels.

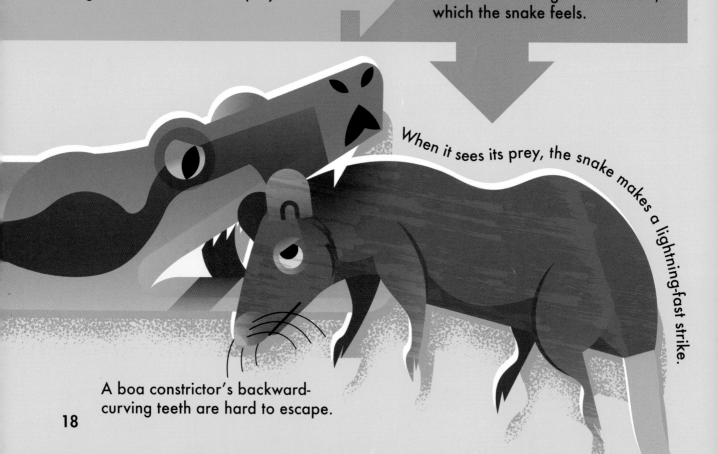

When it sees its prey, the snake makes a lightning-fast strike.

A boa constrictor's backward-curving teeth are hard to escape.

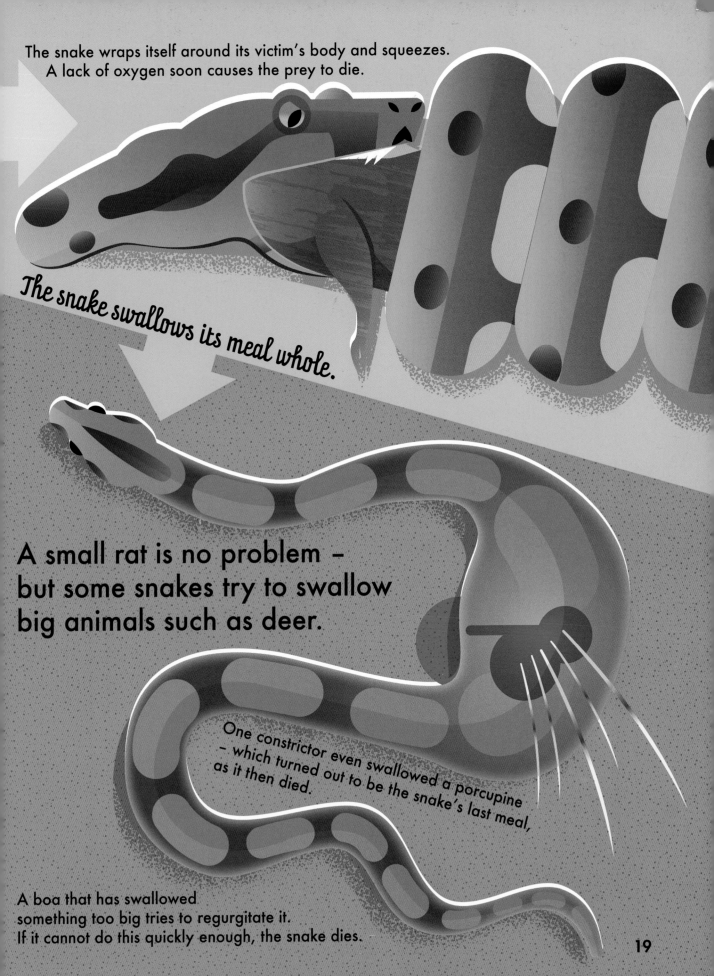

The snake wraps itself around its victim's body and squeezes. A lack of oxygen soon causes the prey to die.

The snake swallows its meal whole.

A small rat is no problem – but some snakes try to swallow big animals such as deer.

One constrictor even swallowed a porcupine – which turned out to be the snake's last meal, as it then died.

A boa that has swallowed something too big tries to regurgitate it. If it cannot do this quickly enough, the snake dies.

Watch Out! Crocodiles About

Every year, wildebeest migrate around the Serengeti plains of Africa in search of fresh grazing.

On their journey, the wildebeest face all kinds of dangers – plus some particularly chaotic river crossings.

In January, the herds head south. Between now and March, their calves will be born.

The survivors make it back to the northern feeding grounds by **August.**
They stay until rains further south cause new grass to grow in **November.**

Because calves are an easy meal, predators follow the herds to the southern Serengeti.

By April and May, the southern grasses are running out. The herds move towards fresh pastures in the central and western Serengeti.

The most dangerous part of their journey is next.

In July, the wildebeest reach the wide, murky rivers of the western Serengeti. Waiting in the waters are hungry Nile crocodiles.

The crossing is chaos!

Even if they make it across, a few wildebeest are dragged back in by the crocodiles.

Although many wildebeest die during the migration, far more would starve if they did not travel to find fresh food.

Moth Love Potion

Like many insects, a moth's life cycle is fascinating. Moths don't start life as moths at all. They go through three other shapes first.

A moth's life is also hazardous. In fact, dangers lurk at every step of the way.

Moths start life as eggs, usually laid on leaves.

Insects and small birds eat the eggs.

Eggs

Any caterpillar that survives becomes a pupa. Pupae are eaten by birds, spiders, frogs, toads and snakes.

Pupa

Caterpillar

Cunning wasps even inject their own eggs into the moth eggs, giving newly hatched wasp grubs something to eat.

The surviving eggs hatch into caterpillars. Birds, mice and some insects all eat moth caterpillars.

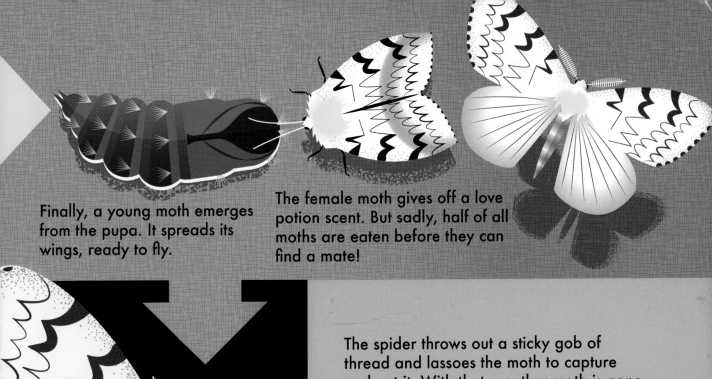

Finally, a young moth emerges from the pupa. It spreads its wings, ready to fly.

The female moth gives off a love potion scent. But sadly, half of all moths are eaten before they can find a mate!

The spider throws out a sticky gob of thread and lassoes the moth to capture and eat it. With that, another moth is gone.

Bolas spider

If a male moth does smell a female it heads in her direction. But the chaos isn't over. Sometimes, the moth love scent is released by a sneaky bolas spider. **Uh-oh ...**

Only one moth egg in 400 manages to become a breeding adult and start the cycle again.

The Tentacled* Terror!

Multi-armed sea monsters that attack sailors don't actually exist – but the giant Pacific octopus does.

This octopus is said to reach an arm span of over 8 m, and weigh three times as much as a grown man. It is also a deadly hunter.

It bites down with its sharp beak.

Sometimes octopuses inject venom into their prey, leaving it unable to move.

At night, the octopus leaves its den and feels its way along the sea floor. Octopus arms have taste buds, so it tastes whatever it touches.

When it touches prey the octopus grabs it, holding on with suckers on its arms.

*We shouldn't really call them tentacles: the proper name is 'arms'.

The octopus heads for a den or safe place to eat.

If a predator such as a shark appears, the octopus changes colour to camouflage itself, or squirts out a cloud of ink.

Sometimes octopuses wave one arm around for predators to bite off. The arm carries on wriggling, the octopus escapes and the arm grows back later.

Overfishing – especially of sharks – means there are fewer predators around, and more octopuses.

The tentacled terrors are **taking over** the oceans, and who knows, maybe they'll crawl onto the land next ... *

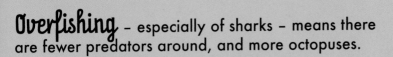

*Don't worry – all octopuses need water to breathe, so they can only stay on land for a short time.

The Cat with a Sore Paw

Cheetahs are the fastest predators on land. In 2012 a cheetah called Sarah was recorded running at almost 100 kph.

Cheetahs are built for speed, not endurance. They need to catch their prey quickly – and that's not the only challenge they face.

The black stripes beside a cheetah's eyes may stop it being dazzled by the sun.

When a cheetah sees prey, it begins to move slowly towards it.

The cheetah aims to creep within 30 m before being spotted.

When the prey runs, the cheetah sprints after it.

Its claws act like spiked running shoes, giving extra grip.

At top speed, the cheetah takes more than three strides per second.

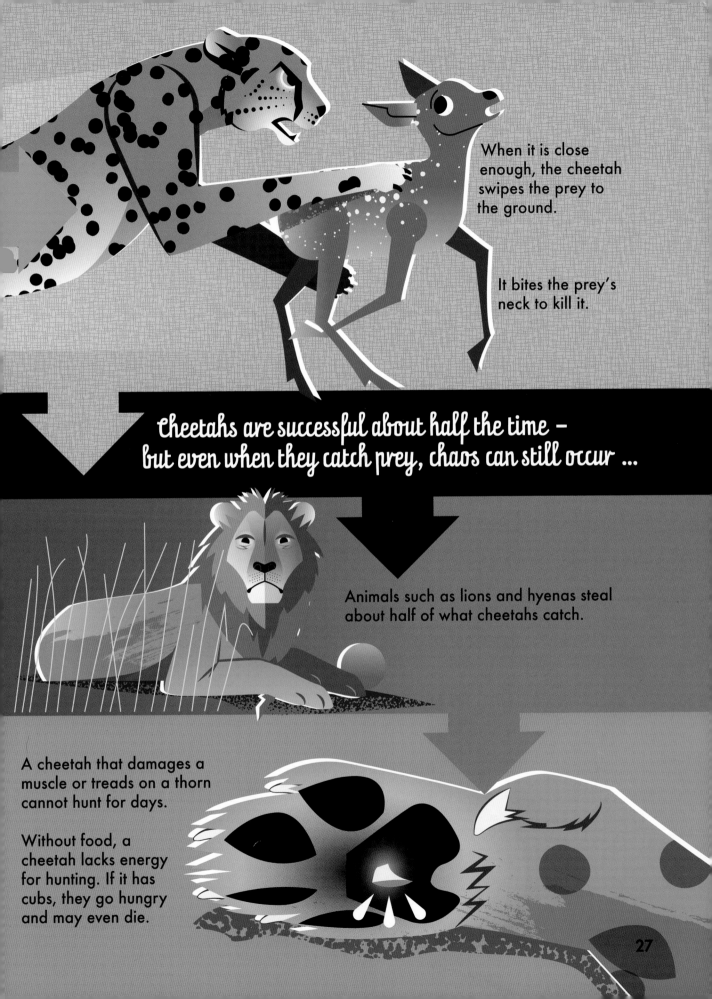

When it is close enough, the cheetah swipes the prey to the ground.

It bites the prey's neck to kill it.

Cheetahs are successful about half the time – but even when they catch prey, chaos can still occur ...

Animals such as lions and hyenas steal about half of what cheetahs catch.

A cheetah that damages a muscle or treads on a thorn cannot hunt for days.

Without food, a cheetah lacks energy for hunting. If it has cubs, they go hungry and may even die.

The Lonely Rhinos

The world is a tough place for wild animals. They are hunted and affected by habitat loss. Some animals have become extinct as a result.

One animal teetering on the brink of extinction is the northern white rhino.

Years ago, thousands of northern white rhinos roamed across central Africa.

Then they began to be hunted as trophies. By 1960 there were only 2,000 left.

During the 1980s, demand increased for rhino horn to use in Chinese and Vietnamese medicine. Rhino horn does not actually have any medicinal value.

Even so, a small pile of ground-down horn became more valuable than gold or diamonds.

Poachers began killing rhinos to saw off their horns for sale.

Poachers have even killed rhinos living in zoos.

Rhino numbers fell dramatically,
and by 2010 no northern white rhinos were left in the wild.

In 2018, the last male northern white rhino died.
Only two females are left.

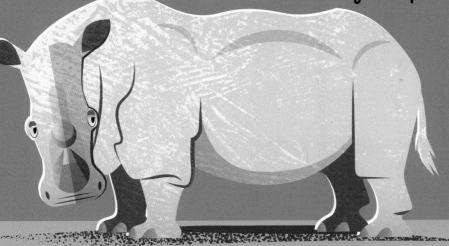

Every extinct species is a **disaster** for the world – species diversity, whether in rhinos, plants or sharks, ensures a balanced eco-system where each lifeform has a role to play. The removal of one species impacts on the life of all surrounding creatures.

Glossary

anticoagulant chemical that makes blood thinner, and stops it forming clots or a scab that seals a cut

apex predator predator at the top of the food chain, which no other animal hunts

breathing hole hole in ice where seals and other animals come to the surface to breathe

burrow underground tunnel in which an animal lives

calf the name for a young cow, wildebeest, buffalo, elephant, whale, etc.

camouflage coloured disguise that blends into the background

carcass dead body

den hiding place or shelter of a wild mammal, such as a fox, bear, mink or stoat

downwind when an animal stands downwind of another animal the scent of that animal blows towards it

endurance ability to do something, such as run, for a long time

extinct die out completely, when one type of animal or plant can no longer be found living on Earth

graze eat grass or other plants

habitat natural home landscape of an animal

habitat loss destruction of a habitat (this usually means destruction that has happened because of human activity)

hibernation time during winter when an animal goes into a deep sleep, slowing its breathing and reducing its body temperature

immobile not able to move

joint connection between two bones, which allows movement. Examples are elbows and knees.

nutrient something that living creatures can use for life and growth

overfishing catching of so many fish that they cannot reproduce quickly enough to replace the ones that have been caught

poacher someone who illegally catches and kills animals

predator an animal that kills and feeds on other animals

regurgitate bring food that has been swallowed back up into the mouth

roost place where birds rest at night

spawn release eggs

suffocate deprive of air, so that the victim dies

venom poisonous substance produced by some animals, such as snakes and spiders

Finding Out More

Animal kingdom places

The Natural History Museum
Cromwell Road
London SW7 5BD
www.nhm.ac.uk

The museum has permanent and temporary exhibitions about the natural world, including mammals, birds, marine reptiles, creepy crawlies and more. Every year, usually in October and November, the museum hosts an exhibition of the best entries in the Wildlife Photographer of the Year competition. For anyone interested in animals, this exhibition makes a visit really worthwhile.

Nature reserves, animal sanctuaries, zoos and safari parks are great places to study a variety of animals. Don't forget to notice animals outside your window, on the street, in gardens, playgrounds, parks and in the countryside.

Animal kingdom books

Animal Kingdom Book of Prints by Millie Marotta (Batsford, 2017)
A beautiful, intricate colouring book with giraffes, birds, octopuses and a bunch of other animals to colour in and create your own unique animal images.

The Big Countdown: Ten Thousand, Eight Hundred and Twenty Endangered Species in the Animal Kingdom by Paul Rockett (Franklin Watts, 2016)
How many black feathers can you expect to find on a pink flamingo? Which are the world's biggest and smallest animals? And could you ever count the fish in the Amazon? For these and other animal-related facts that will amaze and impress your friends, this is the place to look.

World in Infographics: Animal Kingdom by Jon Richards (Wayland, 2014)
Once you start digging into this book it's tough to stop. From the jaw-dropping number of animal species (1.5 million!) to the amazing migrations of monarch butterflies, *Animal Kingdom* is crammed with fascinating facts about the animal world.

Index